CONSERVATIONISTS

SIGURD F. OLSON

JOANNE MATTERN

ABDO Publishing Company

visit us at
www.abdopublishing.com

Printed in the United States of America, North Mankato, Minnesota.
112013
012014

 PRINTED ON RECYCLED PAPER

Cover Photos: Getty Images; iStockphoto
Interior Photos: Corbis p. 26; Getty Images pp. 1, 13, 17; Glow Images pp. 19, 21, 23;
    iStockphoto p. 1; Wisconsin Historical Society, WHS-74066 p. 5; Wisconsin Historical Society,
    WHS-74063 p. 7; Wisconsin Historical Society, WHS-74090 p. 9; Wisconsin Historical Society,
    WHS-63197 p. 11; Wisconsin Historical Society, WHS-74158 p. 15; Wisconsin Historical
    Society, WHS-74072 p. 27

Editors: Rochelle Baltzer, Tamara L. Britton, Bridget O'Brien
Art Direction: Neil Klinepier

Library of Congress Control Number: 2013951992

Cataloging-in-Publication Data

Mattern, Joanne.
 Sigurd F. Olson / Joanne Mattern.
   p. cm. -- (Conservationists)
Includes bibliographical references and index.
ISBN 978-1-62403-095-6
1.Olson, Sigurd F., 1899-1982--Juvenile literature. 2. Naturalists--United States--Biography--
Juvenile literature. 3. Conservationists--United States--Biography--Juvenile literature. 4. Nature
conservation--United States--History--20th century--Biography--Juvenile literature. 1. Title.
333.72092--dc23
[B]

2013951992

CONTENTS

YOUNG NATURALIST

Sigurd F. Olson loved nature. He spent most of his life in the woods and on the rivers of the northern United States. He devoted his life to preserving wild places.

Sigurd Ferdinand Olson was born on April 4, 1899, in Chicago, Illinois. His father, Lawrence Olson, was a Baptist church minister. His mother, Ida May Cederholm Olson, cared for the home and children. Sigurd had an older brother named Kenneth.

When Sigurd was seven years old, his family moved to Sister Bay in Door County, Wisconsin. Door County is on the Door **Peninsula**. It lies between Green Bay and Lake Michigan. Sigurd was surrounded by water and wilderness.

Sigurd spent his time exploring the woods. He studied the water on both sides of the peninsula. He learned to fish and to identify plants and animals. It was here that Sigurd's love for the wilderness began.

The Olsons moved many times during Sigurd's childhood. In 1909, they lived in Prentice, Wisconsin. There, Sigurd (front row, left) attended elementary school.

COLLEGE YEARS

In 1912, the Olson family moved to Ashland, Wisconsin. Ashland is by the shores of Lake Superior. Olson spent a lot of time exploring the lake.

Olson also enjoyed hiking in the woods. He studied birds and other wild animals. He explored nearby forests and rivers. He also learned to trap and hunt. He saved his money and bought his own rifle. He used it to hunt deer.

In 1916, Olson graduated from Ashland High School. Later that year, he entered Northland College. During the summers he worked on the Uhrenholdt family farm. There, he met Elizabeth Uhrenholdt. The two enjoyed spending time together.

In 1918, Olson transferred to the University of Wisconsin in Madison. He graduated in 1920 with a degree in agriculture.

Olson leaves Ashland for the University of Wisconsin.

FUN FACT:

Today, Northland College is the site of the Sigurd Olson Environmental Institute. This organization works to find solutions to environmental issues in the north country.

CANOE COUNTRY

In 1920, Olson got a teaching job in the northern Minnesota towns of Nashwauk and Keewatin. Olson taught animal **husbandry**. He also taught **geology** and agricultural **botany**.

Olson was glad to have found a job in the woods. In June 1921, he took his first canoe trip. As he paddled through the northern Minnesota wilderness, he fell in love with the wild and beautiful country. He decided to write a story about his adventure.

OLSON'S PHILOSOPHY

Sigurd Olson believed that modern life is stressful. He thought that spending time in the wilderness allowed one to regain calmness and balance. He believed that wilderness is necessary for a healthy life.

In July, the *Nashwauk Herald* published "Cruising Through God's Country." Later that month, the article was also published in the *Milwaukee Journal*. It was the first of many **literary** works Olson would write about the wilderness.

Olson paddles his canoe in the northland.

FAMILY MAN

During his college years, Olson had stayed in touch with Elizabeth Uhrenholdt. He had finished school and was working. So they decided to marry.

The wedding was held on August 8, 1921, at the Uhrenholdt farm. Olson wanted to share his love of the wilderness with Elizabeth. So on their honeymoon, they went on a three-week-long canoe trip.

Olson loved being in the woods and lakes that lined the border between the United States and Canada. He wanted to earn a living there that would support a family. Mining was an important part of the area's **economy**. So in 1922, Olson returned to the University of Wisconsin. His goal was a graduate degree in **geology**.

On September 15, 1923, the Olsons welcomed their first son, Sigurd Thorne. Olson left school and got a job teaching at Ely High School in Ely, Minnesota. Two years later, on December 23, 1925, their second son, Robert Keith, was born.

Sigurd and Elizabeth Olson

Saving the Wild

In 1925, Olson discovered that the government wanted to build roads and dams in the Superior National Forest. He thought this was a terrible idea. He and many other people wanted the area to remain wild.

Olson worked to stop development and preserve the area's wilderness. In 1926, Secretary of Agriculture William Jardine allowed only two roads to be built. At the same time, the government created three wilderness areas within the forest.

In addition to his conservation work and position at the high school, Olson was teaching at Ely Junior College. Olson taught animal **biology** and human **physiology**.

Olson enjoyed teaching. But he wanted to develop a career as a nature writer. In 1927, Olson's first magazine article, "Fishin' Jewelry," was published in *Field & Stream* magazine.

FUN FACT:

In the United States, a wilderness area is land that is preserved and protected by law in its natural condition. There are 757 wilderness areas, but they protect only 5 percent of the land.

In 1909, the Superior National Forest was created in Minnesota. In 1913,
Canada's Quetico Provincial Park was formed in Ontario. Together, these parks
form the area known as Quetico-Superior.

OUTDOORSMAN

Olson was happiest when he was outdoors. During the summers, he worked as a guide for an **outfitter**. It was the perfect job for him. So in 1929, he and two other men started Border Lakes Outfitting Company. Olson was active in the company for more than 20 years.

Olson realized a graduate degree would give him more opportunities for outdoor work. He decided to return to school and complete his graduate program. But Olson had decided against a career in the mining industry. He did not want to destroy the land.

In 1931, the family moved to Champaign, Illinois. Olson studied **zoology** at the University of Illinois. When he graduated in 1932, the family moved back to Ely.

Olson returned to teaching at Ely Junior College. He also continued working on his writing career. In 1932, *Sports Afield* published "Search for the Wild." In this article, Olson wrote about how important wilderness was to him. In 1936, he was named the college's **dean**.

The Shack is a small building behind the Olson house in Ely. Olson did his writing there.

CONSERVATIONIST

In 1938, the three wilderness areas in the Superior National Forest were named the Superior Roadless Areas. That same year, *American Forests* published "Why Wilderness?" It was Olson's first article published in a conservation magazine.

A big step in Olson's writing career came in 1941. He got a **syndicated** newspaper column. In "America Out of Doors" Olson shared his views about nature with a wider audience. In 1947, Olson left teaching to become a full-time writer and conservationist.

The following year, Olson led a successful fight to ban airplanes from the northern Minnesota wilderness. The work brought him national attention. He became one of the country's best-known conservationists.

However, his work was less popular at home. There were resorts in the area that could only be reached by plane. In addition, Ely had the world's largest float plane base. The airplane ban threatened the livelihoods of those who owned and worked at these businesses.

Quetico-Superior is far north and away from bright city lights.
So visitors often see the aurora borealis, or northern lights.

WRITING SUCCESS

Olson was not discouraged from his work. In 1953, he became president of the National Parks Association. Three years later, he published his first book, *The Singing Wilderness*. The book expressed Olson's experiences and feelings about nature. Readers loved his beautiful **imagery**. The book became a *New York Times* best seller.

That same year, Olson was elected to the Wilderness Society's governing board. Fellow member Howard Zahniser was working on a law. It would create a national system to preserve wilderness places. Olson helped write it.

In 1958, the Superior Roadless Areas became the Boundary Waters Canoe Area (BWCA). That same year, Olson's next book, *Listening Point*, was published. The book's title was the name of a cabin the Olsons had built on Burntside Lake near Ely in 1956.

Olson worked with the National Parks Association until 1959. Then, he joined the advisory board of the National Park Service. In 1963, he became vice president of the Wilderness Society.

In 1962, developers wanted to build houses on California's Point Reyes Peninsula. Olson worked with the National Parks Association to preserve the area as Point Reyes National Seashore.

NATIONAL REACH

The law that Olson and Zahniser worked on had been moving through Congress for eight long years. Finally in 1964, President Lyndon B. Johnson signed the Wilderness Act. This law established the U.S. Wilderness Preservation System.

In 1965, Olson joined a National Park Service task force. The group recommended preserving almost 80 million acres (32,374,851 ha) of Alaskan wilderness. Olson felt that preserving Alaska was the most important battle facing conservationists.

Government officials knew that many people would not agree. They would fear losing their land and livelihoods. So the report was kept secret for many years.

However in 1980, the work Olson and the other members did led to the Alaska National Interest Lands and Conservation Act. This law preserved millions of acres of Alaskan land. The Arctic National Wildlife Refuge (ANWR) was part of the land preserved by the law.

CONSERVATION ALERT!
In the United States, 6,000 acres (2,428 ha) of open space is lost to development each day.

A polar bear's den. The highest population of polar bear land dens is in the ANWR.

A polar bear mother nurses her cub. Besides habitat destruction, melting sea ice and pollution threaten their survival.

NATIONAL PARK

By the 1970s, Olson's writing career was well established. In addition, he had received awards from most of the large conservation organizations in America. This included the Sierra Club and the National Wildlife Federation.

One of Olson's goals was to create a wilderness area in northern Minnesota. In 1971, President Richard Nixon signed a law that established Voyageurs National Park. Olson was honored when he was asked to choose the park's name.

That same year, Olson and Senator Gaylord Nelson, who had helped create Earth Day, led a conference at Northland College in Ashland, Wisconsin. After the conference, Northland established the Sigurd Olson Environmental Institute.

FUN FACT:

In 1974, Olson received the John Burroughs Medal for his book Wilderness Days. *This is the highest honor for nature writing.*

Voyageurs National Park preserves 218,054 acres (88,243 ha) of wilderness. It is the state of Minnesota's only national park.

BWCAW

During this time, Congress was debating the Boundary Waters Canoe Area Wilderness Act. If it became law, the act would expand the BWCA by about 50,000 acres (20,234 ha). Many people would lose privately held land. The law would also ban logging and mining in the area.

Not everyone was happy about these conservation efforts. Tourism was an important part of Ely's **economy**. Some citizens believed that the new regulations would keep tourists out of the area. They had not forgotten the airplane ban that had caused resorts to lose business.

Citizens who were against the law protested. Some blamed Olson. In 1977, protestors hanged a representation of Olson to express their anger at him.

But in 1978, President Jimmy Carter signed the Boundary Waters Canoe Area Wilderness Act. The law made the BWCA a wilderness area. It became the Boundary Waters Canoe Area Wilderness (BWCAW). Olson's dream for preserving the Quetico-Superior area had come true.

MANITOBA

CANADA

ONTARIO

Quetico Provincial
Park

Voyageurs National Park

Boundary Waters Canoe
Area Wilderness

●Ely

Lake
Superior

Superior National Forest

NORTH
DAKOTA

MINNESOTA

WISCONSIN

United States

↑
N

FUN FACT:

The BWCAW preserves 1.1 million acres (445,154 ha) of wilderness.

LASTING LEGACY

Olson had work outdoors that he loved. He helped craft laws that preserved millions of acres of wilderness. His nine books and countless articles gave him an opportunity to express his **philosophy** on the importance of wilderness.

On January 13, 1982, Olson died of a heart attack while snowshoeing near his Ely home. He was 82 years old.

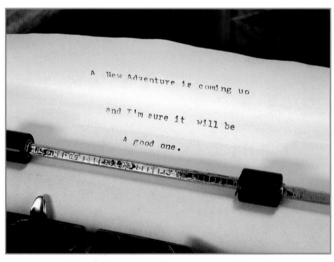

Olson's last words were typed on his typewriter in The Shack.

Olson always did what he thought was best for the wilderness. He was proud of his achievements. He believed the sacrifices made were worth it. Today, his work lives on in the wilderness areas he loved so much and worked so hard to conserve.

Olson at Listening Point. The cabin was placed on the National Register of Historic Places in 2007.

TIMELINE

1899 Sigurd Ferdinand Olson was born on April 4 in Chicago, Illinois.

1912 The Olson family moved to Ashland, Wisconsin.

1916 Olson graduated from high school; he entered Northland College.

1918 Olson transferred to the University of Wisconsin in Madison; two years later he graduated with a degree in agriculture.

1921 On August 8, Olson married Elizabeth Uhrenholdt.

1923 Son Sigurd Thorne Olson was born on September 15.

1925 Olson limited development in Superior National Forest; son Robert Keith Olson was born on December 23.

1927 Olson's first magazine article was published.

1931 The family moved to Champaign, Illinois, where Olson studied at the University of Illinois; he graduated the following year with a degree in zoology.

1936 Olson became dean of Ely Junior College.

1941 Olson's syndicated newspaper column began.

1948 ●	Olson's work to have airplanes banned in the Quetico-Superior area succeeded.
1956 ●	*The Singing Wilderness* was published; the Olsons built the cabin they named Listening Point.
1958 ●	The Boundary Waters Canoe Area was established; *Listening Point* was published.
1964 ●	The Wilderness Act passed.
1971 ●	Voyageurs National Park was established.
1978 ●	The Boundary Waters Canoe Area Wilderness Act passed.
1982 ●	Olson died on January 13 in Ely, Minnesota.

"Unless we can preserve places where the endless spiritual needs of man can be fulfilled and nourished, we will destroy our culture and ourselves."

—Sigurd F. Olson

GLOSSARY

biology - the study of living things, especially plants and animals. A scientist who studies biology is a biologist.

botany - the study of plant life. A scientist who studies botany is a botanist.

dean - a person at a college or university who is in charge of guiding students.

economy - the way a nation produces and uses goods, services, and natural resources.

geology - the science of Earth and its structure. A person who studies geology is called a geologist.

husbandry - the breeding, raising, and management of livestock.

imagery - language in a story that causes readers to imagine pictures in their minds.

literary - of or relating to books or literature.

outfitter - a business that provides equipment, supplies, and trained guidance especially on hunting and fishing trips.

peninsula - land that sticks out into water and is connected to a larger landmass.

philosophy (fuh-LAH-suh-fee) - a set of ideas about knowledge and truth.

physiology (fih-zee-AH-luh-jee) - a branch of biology dealing with the normal functions of living things. A physiologist studies the processes and activities by which life is carried on.

syndicate (SIHN-duh-kayt) - to sell something for publication in many newspapers or magazines at the same time.

zoology (zoh-AH-luh-jee) - a branch of biology that deals with animals and their behavior. A scientist who studies zoology is a zoologist.

WEB SITES

To learn more about Sigurd F. Olson, visit ABDO Publishing Company online. Web sites about Sigurd F. Olson are featured on our Book Links page. These links are routinely monitored and updated to provide the most current information available.
www.abdopublishing.com

INDEX